WHAT IS ARTIFICIAL INTELLIGENCE?

by Kathryn Hulick

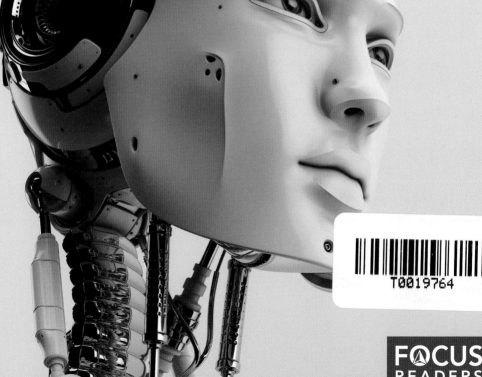

T0019764

FOCUS
READERS.

VOYAGER

www.focusreaders.com

Focus Readers is distributed by North Star Editions:
sales@northstareditions.com | 888-417-0195

Produced for Focus Readers by Red Line Editorial.

Content Consultant: Dr. James W. Davis, Professor, Department of Computer Science & Engineering, Ohio State University

Photographs ©: Ociacia/Shutterstock Images, cover, 1; Gregor Fischer/picture-alliance/dpa/AP Images, 4–5; oneinchpunch/Shutterstock Images, 7; Sk Hasan Ali/Shutterstock Images, 8; Lenscap Photography/Shutterstock Images, 11; Robert Kaiser/File/AP Images, 12–13; kate_sept2004/iStockphoto, 14; indypendenZ/iStockphoto, 16–17; plenoy m/Shutterstock Images, 19; Adam Nadel/AP Images, 21; Dmytro Zinkevych/Shutterstock Images, 22–23; David M. Phillips/Science Source, 25; Red Line Editorial, 27, 31 (infographic), 41; ivansmuk/iStockphoto, 28–29; Nadya_Art/Shutterstock Images, 31 (dogs); Zapp2Photo/Shutterstock Images, 33; Matt Winkelmeyer/Wired 25/Getty Images Entertainment/Getty Images, 35; Keith Srakocic/AP Images, 36–37; Science Picture Co/Science Source, 39; Prykhodov/iStockphoto, 42–43; Seth Wenig/AP Images, 45

Library of Congress Cataloging-in-Publication Data
Names: Hulick, Kathryn, author.
Title: What is artificial intelligence? / by Kathryn Hulick.
Description: Lake Elmo, MN : Focus Readers, 2020. | Series: Artificial
   intelligence | Includes index. | Audience: Grades 7–9.
Identifiers: LCCN 2019032748 (print) | LCCN 2019032749 (ebook) | ISBN
   9781644930762 (hardcover) | ISBN 9781644931554 (paperback) | ISBN
   9781644933138 (pdf) | ISBN 9781644932346 (ebook)
Subjects: LCSH: Artificial intelligence--Juvenile literature.
Classification: LCC Q335.4 .H853 2020 (print) | LCC Q335.4 (ebook) | DDC
   006.3--dc23
LC record available at https://lccn.loc.gov/2019032748
LC ebook record available at https://lccn.loc.gov/2019032749

Printed in the United States of America
Mankato, MN
012020

ABOUT THE AUTHOR

Kathryn Hulick began her career with an adventure. She served two years in the Peace Corps in Kyrgyzstan, teaching English. When she returned to the United States, she began writing books and articles for kids. She also contributes regularly to *Muse* magazine and the Science News for Students website. Artificial intelligence and robots are her two favorite topics. She enjoys hiking, painting, reading, and working in her garden. She lives in Massachusetts with her husband, son, and dog.

TABLE OF CONTENTS

CHAPTER 1

PASSING THE TEST

A judge sat at a computer, typing back and forth with two unknown partners. One partner was human. The other was a computer program called a **chatbot**. The judge was trying to figure out which was which. One of the partners, named Mitsuku, told the judge that she enjoys learning about everything. Later, the judge asked Mitsuku what she was thinking about. She answered that she was thinking about their conversation.

Humans can have conversations with computer programs called chatbots.

She said she was giving it her full attention. But could Mitsuku really think or pay attention? She could not. She was the chatbot.

Mitsuku is an example of artificial intelligence (AI). An AI is a smart machine, typically a robot or a computer **algorithm**. The term AI also refers to the science and engineering of smart machines. AI programs can solve problems or perform tasks that normally require human thought and intelligence.

Mitsuku was competing for the 2018 Loebner Prize. It is a yearly contest that tests AI. It is also an example of a Turing test. An AI program passes the Turing test if it can convince human judges that it is human. Hugh Loebner, a businessperson, offered a $100,000 prize and a gold medal to the first AI program to do this. But as of 2018, no chatbots had claimed the gold or even the silver

△ People can interact with AI chatbots on their smartphones.

medal. Most of the judges figured out Mitsuku was not human. She sometimes made very bizarre statements. But Mitsuku outperformed all of the other chatbots in the competition. So she won a bronze medal for the fourth time.

Other AI programs have tried to pass as people. In 2014, a chatbot posing as a 13-year-old boy named Eugene Goostman won a competition similar to the Loebner Prize. Some people even claimed the program had passed the Turing test.

The robot Sophia responds to a question during the 2017 Digital World expo in Dhaka, Bangladesh.

But the chatbot used tricks. It pretended to be a child from Ukraine who didn't speak very good English. It changed the subject and made jokes. These tricks fooled some judges. In 2017, a robot named Sophia became a citizen of the country of Saudi Arabia. Sophia can express emotions with her human-like features. But her programmers plan out many of the things she says.

Mitsuku, Eugene, and Sophia do not really understand human language. They are not self-aware or conscious in the way that people are. But many experts say that's beside the point. Intelligence is really about the ability to learn and solve problems. AI already solves many problems that are time-consuming and difficult for people. AI powers **virtual** assistants such as Siri and Alexa. It offers up search engine results, translates languages, and diagnoses diseases. In the future, AI will only become smarter. The "mind" of an AI program may never work exactly like a human's brain. So AI may never pass as human. But it can still accomplish amazing things.

THINK ABOUT IT ◄

People have wondered if machines might someday think. What is your opinion? Can today's AI programs already think? How might their thinking differ from yours?

ALAN TURING

Alan Turing was a British mathematician and one of the very first computer scientists. During World War II (1939–1945), he built a machine called the Bombe. It could decipher the complex Enigma code that the Nazis used. He received high honors for his service to his country.

After the war, Turing helped start the field of computer science. He did his groundbreaking research at the National Physical Laboratory in London and later at Manchester University. In 1950, he wondered if machines might be able to think someday. But the word "think" was too hard to define. So he came up with another question. He wondered if a machine might ever win the imitation game. In the game, a machine chats with a human judge. If the judge thinks the machine is human, it wins the game. Today, this

Bletchley Park, where British and Allied codebreakers worked during World War II, has a statue of Alan Turing.

game is known as the Turing test. It is Turing's most famous contribution to the field of AI.

Turing had many other important ideas about AI. He predicted that intelligent machines would be able to learn from experience. And he realized these machines would someday take over some human jobs. His predictions have proven true.

CHAPTER 2

THE EARLY YEARS OF AI

In 1956, the Dartmouth Summer Research Project on Artificial Intelligence took place. Participants had bold plans for the new field of AI. They wanted to build machines that could learn, use human language, observe the world, and more. All of these goals proved to be very difficult. Computer technology at the time was very costly and slow. But the US government wanted AI, especially for translation and **transcription**.

Marvin Minsky is considered one of the pioneers in the field of AI.

▲ Early robots struggled to pick things up, an ability human toddlers gain by trial and error.

So, the Defense Advanced Research Projects Agency gave out millions of dollars to researchers.

In the 1960s, researchers developed the first chatbot. ELIZA talked like a human therapist. It used only 200 lines of code. It followed simple patterns to respond to people's statements with questions. In 1966, Shakey became the first robot that could map its surroundings and move on its own. But it could only move through a carefully constructed room. And it moved very slowly.

By 1970, researchers were frustrated. AI wasn't progressing as quickly as they'd hoped. Computers could easily perform complex math. But they couldn't do things that were simple for two-year-olds, such as walking or seeing. In 1980, robotics expert Hans Moravec pointed out that in computer science, hard problems are easy and easy problems are hard. His explanation was that humans evolved the abilities to see and move over millions of years. People also develop common sense just by living in the world. Machines didn't evolve or spend years experiencing the world. They had to start from scratch.

THINK ABOUT IT ◀

Do you think it would be easier for robots to plan winning chess moves or to pick up and move chess pieces? Which would be easier for you? Why?

CHAPTER 3

FOLLOWING THE RULES

Logical rules guided most early AI algorithms through solving problems. One type of logical rule is the if-then statement. For example, a developer might program a robot with the rule, "If an obstacle is in front of you, then do not move forward." This programming method is known as top-down or symbolic AI.

A chatbot that uses top-down AI would be given a dictionary of words and their definitions.

Developers can program AI to follow certain rules.

It would also have a set of grammar rules to help it handle sentences. The 1970 program SHRDLU worked this way. It could have simple conversations with users. It broke the user's sentences apart. Then it defined each word. It could only talk about a simple, virtual world of blocks. Top-down AI for language processing and translation improved over the years. But it never came close to human-like conversation.

AI algorithms called expert systems follow a top-down approach to solve specific problems. They start with a collection of facts called a knowledge base. And they use logical rules to

> ## ➤ THINK ABOUT IT

What logical rules might you use to program a computer to play tic-tac-toe? Try using if-then statements to describe the game.

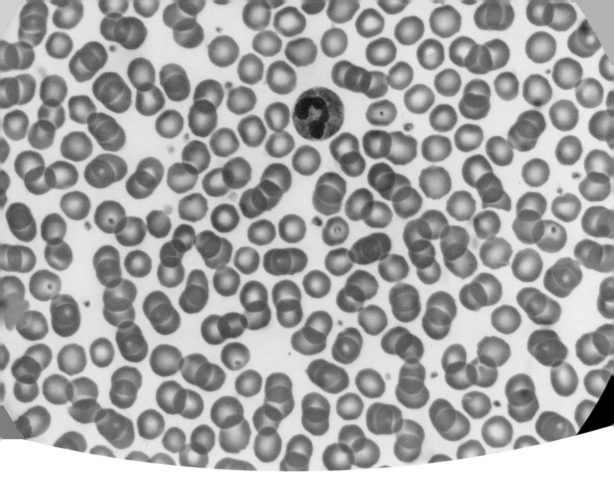

▲ Expert systems have been used to analyze blood samples and identify the presence of infection.

make inferences using those facts. For example, the expert system MYCIN was developed in the 1970s. It could diagnose blood infections and suggest treatments. It followed approximately 500 rules. The algorithm performed as well as human specialists.

Expert systems became popular in the 1980s. The credit-card company American Express used one to decide whether to give customers credit. Airlines used the technology for scheduling and to plan repairs.

Top-down AI also succeeded at solving logic puzzles and playing games. In May 1997, the algorithm Deep Blue beat Garry Kasparov, the best human chess player. The algorithm followed logical rules. It could run through 200 million possible future states of the chess board every second. Then it would pick the move that was most likely to result in a win.

However, there was one big problem with the top-down approach. Programmers had to completely describe the problem at hand. The algorithms couldn't easily handle new, unexpected situations. This wasn't a big deal for

▲ Garry Kasparov (left) considers the board during his
1997 chess match against Deep Blue.

playing chess. The game has clear rules that do
not change. But the real world is vast, messy, and
constantly changing. For example, programmers
can't plan for every single situation in which a
moving robot might end up. To function in the
real world, AI programs needed to be able to
experience the real world. They also needed to be
able to learn from this experience.

CHAPTER 4

BUILDING A BRAIN

People aren't born with intelligence. A newborn baby can't talk or walk. But the baby has a brain. And that brain has an amazing ability to learn. Every time the baby moves its legs, the brain gets better at planning the movements. Every time the baby hears words, the brain gets better at recognizing them. No one ever gives a baby a set of rules on how to walk or talk. But the baby figures it out anyway.

A baby's brain learns from every experience or interaction the baby has.

Some AI algorithms also figure things out through experience. This process is called machine learning. Machine learning is a bottom-up approach to AI. In this approach, programmers do not write general rules. Instead, they feed an algorithm experiences or examples. Suppose an algorithm needs to translate words from Chinese to English. Its programmers do not have to give it a dictionary. Instead, they can gather many texts written in both languages. A machine-learning algorithm can use these examples to learn which Chinese phrases match which English phrases.

➤ THINK ABOUT IT

Suppose a robot needs to walk without falling over. Would the robot have more success if it was given general rules, or if it learned from experience? Why?

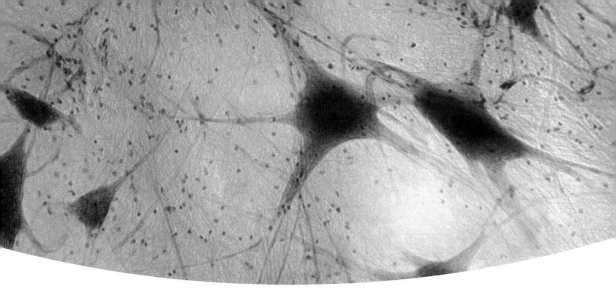

▲ Researchers modeled machine learning after neural connections in the human brain.

Some of the first researchers to work on machine learning looked to the human brain for inspiration. The brain contains approximately 100 billion cells called **neurons**. These neurons link together to form trillions of connections. Groups of connected neurons are called neural networks. They allow the brain to understand and respond to information. Shapes, words, emotions, and other sensations cause patterns of connected neurons to activate. As the brain learns, old patterns change and new patterns emerge.

In 1957, psychologist Frank Rosenblatt came up with a mathematical model. It was a simple artificial neuron. Like a neuron in the brain, it responds differently to different inputs. The connections or links between the inputs and the neuron can be strengthened or weakened. The "weight" of a connection determines its influence on the output of the neuron. These weights are considered the "memory" of the neuron.

An **artificial neural network (ANN)** contains many neurons placed in multiple layers. Each neuron in a layer responds in its own way to its input. The neuron's output becomes the input for neurons in the next layer. The last layer provides a final output. For example, if the input is a Chinese word, the final output might be an English word.

At first, the weights of an ANN are all random. The ANN can only guess the right English word.

But during training, it can adapt its weights. Based on its mistakes, it can use an algorithm to slightly change the weights of its connections or links in order to help correct its errors. In this way, the ANN can learn to give the right answer.

At first, people could only build fairly simple ANNs containing just one or two layers. Larger networks required too much computer power. But over time, people developed more complex ANNs.

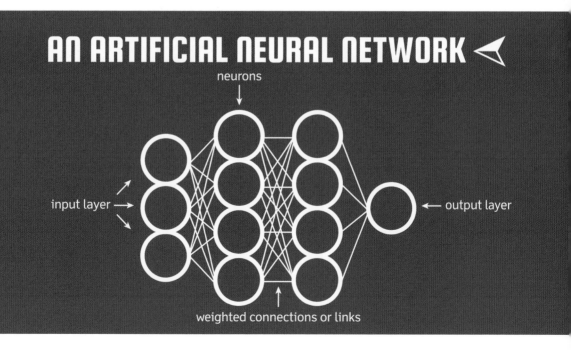

AN ARTIFICIAL NEURAL NETWORK ◄

neurons

input layer →

← output layer

weighted connections or links

CHAPTER 5

DEEP LEARNING

People can easily pick out dogs, airplanes, and other items in photographs. Until recently, computers couldn't do this very well. A contest pitted machine-learning algorithms against one another. They had to identify the objects in photographs. The algorithm that made the fewest mistakes won. In 2010 and 2011, the best algorithms made incorrect decisions on at least 25 percent of images.

The ImageNet contest tested algorithms' ability to recognize the objects in photographs.

In 2012, one algorithm stood out. It made mistakes on only 13 to 14 percent of images. It was nearly twice as good as all of its competitors. Geoffrey Hinton and two of his students at the University of Toronto in Canada made the algorithm. It used an ANN with eight layers. Because it had so many layers, the **technique** was known as **deep learning**.

Back in 1990, computer scientist Yann LeCun had made one of the first successful deep neural networks. It could identify letters and numbers in people's handwriting. The ANN contained just four layers and approximately 98,000 connections. Computers at the time couldn't handle more.

But bigger networks are almost always better. In general, adding more layers and more connections makes a neural network smarter. In 2009, computer scientist Andrew Ng found a solution to enhance computers' processing power.

It was a new computer chip that could process

high-quality images in a fast-paced video game.

It could also process complex neural networks.

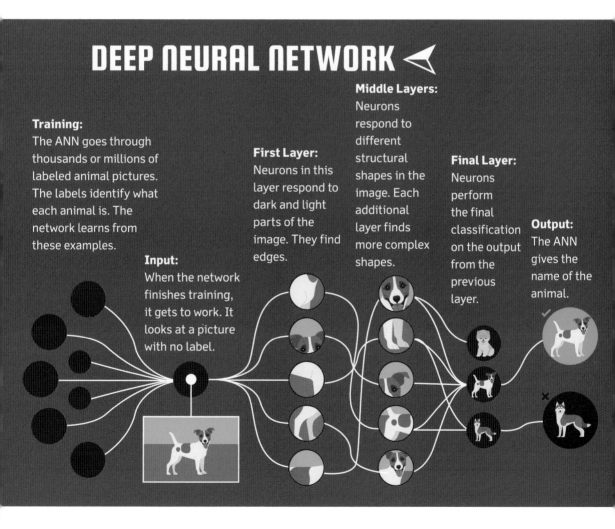

DEEP NEURAL NETWORK

Training:
The ANN goes through thousands or millions of labeled animal pictures. The labels identify what each animal is. The network learns from these examples.

Input:
When the network finishes training, it gets to work. It looks at a picture with no label.

First Layer:
Neurons in this layer respond to dark and light parts of the image. They find edges.

Middle Layers:
Neurons respond to different structural shapes in the image. Each additional layer finds more complex shapes.

Final Layer:
Neurons perform the final classification on the output from the previous layer.

Output:
The ANN gives the name of the animal.

So, it helped networks get bigger. The network Hinton's team made had more than 62 million connections. Today, the largest ANNs have more than 100 billion. But this is still nowhere near the human brain's many trillions of connections.

Deep learning led to huge improvements in many areas of AI. Algorithms got much better at turning speech into text or text into speech. They also improved at translation. Google Translate began using a deep-learning algorithm in 2016. Users noticed a big difference. Overnight, the system improved as much as it had in the previous decade.

Today, AI algorithms such as Facebook's DeepFace are as good as or better than humans at recognizing faces. Google's RankBrain figures out what people really want in their search results. Some self-driving cars and robots use deep

▲ Some AI algorithms learn to recognize faces in photographs.

learning to **navigate**. Doctors are using deep learning to detect diseases. The deep-learning program AlphaGo mastered the challenging game of Go in 2016. And the object-identification challenge ended in 2017 after algorithms had become better than humans at identifying pictures. Hinton said that computer scientists used to think neural networks were a crazy idea. But now, the crazy approach is winning.

FEI-FEI LI

Deep learning was a major breakthrough for AI. But even the biggest deep-learning algorithm can do nothing all by itself. It has to train. And training requires a huge amount of data. That data also has to be of high quality. Learning algorithms will fail if they train on bad examples.

Fei-Fei Li, a computer scientist at Stanford University, began working on a new data set in 2006. She called it ImageNet. Her goal was to map the entire world of objects. ImageNet would be like a visual dictionary for computers.

Li started with an existing data set of words called WordNet. The words were nested into categories. For example, dog breeds such as "Dalmatian" were nested under the category "dog." Li wanted each category to have many sample pictures. But labeling millions of pictures wasn't easy. Her team hired people around the

Fei-Fei Li (right) discusses what's next for AI at the 2018 Wired25 Summit in San Francisco, California.

world to help. The project took several years. When it was done, ImageNet had 3.2 million images divided into more than 5,000 categories.

Many AI developers use ImageNet to train their algorithms for image-related tasks. Li made the data set open and free for anyone to use. And it is still growing. Today, ImageNet has more than 14 million pictures in more than 20,000 categories. Thanks to Li's work, developers now realize how important training data is to an AI program that learns. It is just as important as the algorithm itself.

CHAPTER 6

EVOLVING ROBOTS AND BEYOND

Deep learning is just one example of machine learning. It works best when a lot of training data is available. But that isn't always the case. For example, in 2011, an AI program named Watson defeated the human champions at the quiz game *Jeopardy!* The company IBM built Watson. The developers experimented with deep learning. However, it didn't work well. They didn't have enough examples for training.

Watson faces off against university students in a version of *Jeopardy!* in 2011.

The developers wound up using many different techniques instead. A rules-based algorithm divided up the words in the quiz question. A search engine combed through possible answers. Then, another search gathered evidence for each answer. Still more algorithms gave each answer a score. Finally, a machine-learning algorithm figured out how to merge all the scores and pick the best answer. This algorithm used a math technique from the field of **statistics**.

Evolutionary algorithms are another type of machine-learning technique. They are based on the natural process of **evolution**. Evolution happens when animals' bodies change slowly over many generations. Evolutionary algorithms work in a similar way. They construct a model by slowly making changes over time. They are especially helpful in robotics and engineering. In robotics,

Biological evolution can take millions of years. Evolutionary algorithms can change much more quickly.

evolutionary algorithms can help a robot learn how to move.

The AI system starts out with the pieces it needs to solve a problem. For example, suppose a robot needs to learn how to walk. The robot starts out with motors in its legs and a sensor that tells it if it has fallen over or gotten stuck. Next, the system tries out a random combination of movements. The robot might try moving only its front legs. Or it might twist and fall over.

After many random combinations, the system picks the ones that brought it closest to the goal. In the robot's case, moving the front legs worked better than twisting. The system combines this method with other successful methods. It also introduces some new random changes as well. It tests all of these new methods again. The system repeats this process until one method gives a satisfactory solution to the problem.

NASA engineers used an evolutionary process to design a small antenna for use in space. Small antennas only work well if bent into a complex shape. So, engineers used an evolutionary algorithm to design and test many different shapes to find the best one. A group of three small satellites in the Space Technology 5 mission used the antenna to communicate. Evolutionary algorithms are not as popular today as deep learning or statistical techniques. It can be tricky for developers to figure out how to produce and test the best solutions to a given problem. But the technique may become more popular over time.

TYPES OF AI ◄

Artificial intelligence includes any technique that allows machines to do tasks that normally require human intelligence.
- ELIZA
- Shakey the robot
- Expert systems
- Deep Blue
- Video game characters

Machine learning includes any AI technique that improves with experience or examples.
- Mitsuku chatbot
- Watson
- Evolved antenna
- Netflix recommendations
- Email spam filter

Deep learning includes any machine-learning technique inspired by neural networks in the human brain.
- AlphaGo
- Google Translate
- Google's RankBrain
- Facebook's DeepFace
- Tesla Autopilot (self-driving mode)

CHAPTER 7

SMARTER AND SMARTER

In the near future, AI will grow smarter and more powerful. Meanwhile, the Internet of Things (IoT) is coming into existence. The IoT is a network of real things, such as clothing, appliances, cars, and more. They all collect and share data. People and companies will also continue to gather and save loads of data, such as pictures, video, and text. All of this data will help train machine-learning algorithms.

With the Internet of Things, household electronics can all be connected.

Computer technology will also improve. Better, faster computers mean stronger, smarter AI. Engineers are putting neural networks directly into computer chips. Also, quantum computing promises to greatly increase computer power. In a traditional computer, a bit is the smallest unit of data. It holds a single value, 1 or 0. A qubit in a quantum computer can hold 1 or 0 or both at the same time. So, qubits can do more than one thing at once. IBM predicts that quantum computers will become mainstream by the mid-2020s.

Today's AI algorithms are all designed for a specific purpose. For example, an AI program may translate languages. But that same system can't learn to compose music. In contrast, an AI program that could learn any task as well as a person would have Artificial General Intelligence, or AGI. If an AGI could learn any task

▲ Experts predict quantum computing will lead to many new breakthroughs in machine learning and AI in general.

much better than a person, it would become a superintelligence.

Some experts think AGI and superintelligence will never arise. Others think they may be just a few decades away. The true power of AI, though, is in how it enhances human abilities. With the help of AI, people can improve their lives. Together, humans and machines can do amazing things.

FOCUS ON
ARTIFICIAL INTELLIGENCE

Write your answers on a separate piece of paper.

1. Write a paragraph describing the difference between top-down and bottom-up AI.

2. Would you want computers or robots to become much more intelligent than humans? Why or why not?

3. What is deep learning?

      A. any intelligent computer or robot

      B. a rule-based algorithm

      C. a neural network with many layers

4. For which task would an evolutionary algorithm be most helpful?

      A. playing chess

      B. designing a flying robot

      C. translating languages

Answer key on page 48.

GLOSSARY

algorithm
A set of steps that a computer must follow to complete a process.

artificial neural network (ANN)
An algorithm that learns from data using layers of interconnected units similar to neurons in the brain.

chatbot
An algorithm that talks to people.

deep learning
An AI technique that uses an artificial neural network with three or more layers.

evolution
A process that improves something gradually by making small changes over many generations.

navigate
To find one's way while traveling.

neurons
Brain cells. Networks of connected neurons form thoughts and emotions and control the body.

statistics
A branch of mathematics focused on finding patterns in data.

technique
A method for carrying out a task.

transcription
The process of writing down the words someone says.

virtual
Not existing in reality.

TO LEARN MORE

BOOKS

Hulick, Kathryn. *Artificial Intelligence.* Minneapolis: Abdo Publishing, 2016.

Jackson, Tom. *Will Robots Ever Be Smarter Than Humans? Theories About Artificial Intelligence.* New York: Gareth Stevens Publishing, 2019.

McPherson, Stephanie Sammartino. *Artificial Intelligence: Building Smarter Machines.* Minneapolis: Twenty-First Century Books, 2018.

NOTE TO EDUCATORS

Visit **www.focusreaders.com** to find lesson plans, activities, links, and other resources related to this title.

INDEX

Answer Key: 1. Answers will vary; **2.** Answers will vary; **3.** C; **4.** B